D0821510

Pebble® Plus
Bilingüe/Bilingual

Una visita a/A Visit to

La huerta de manzanas/The Apple Orchard

por/by Patricia J. Murphy

Editor Consultor/Consulting Editor: Dra. Gail Saunders-Smith

Consultor/Consultant: Jennifer Norford, Senior Consultant
Mid-continent Research for Education and Learning
Aurora, Colorado

STAYTON PUBLIC LIBRARY
515 N. 1st Avenue
Stayton, OR 97383

Capstone
press®

Mankato, Minnesota

Pebble Plus is published by Capstone Press
151 Good Counsel Drive, P.O. Box 669, Mankato, Minnesota 56002.
www.capstonepress.com

Copyright © 2008 by Capstone Press, a Coughlan Publishing company. All rights reserved.
No part of this publication may be reproduced in whole or in part, or stored in a retrieval system, or
transmitted in any form or by any means, electronic, mechanical, photocopying, recording, or otherwise,
without written permission of the publisher. For information regarding permission,
write to Capstone Press, 151 Good Counsel Drive, P.O. Box 669, Dept. R, Mankato, Minnesota 56002.
Printed in the United States of America

1 2 3 4 5 6 12 11 10 09 08 07

Library of Congress Cataloging-in-Publication Data
Murphy, Patricia J., 1963–
 [Apple orchard. Spanish & English]
 La huerta de manzanas = The apple orchard / por / by Patricia J. Murphy.
 p. cm.—(Una visita a / A visit to)
 Includes index.
 ISBN-13: 978-1-4296-0081-1 (hardcover : alk. paper)
 ISBN-10: 1-4296-0081-0 (hardcover : alk. paper)
 ISBN-13: 978-1-4296-1194-7 (softcover pbk.)
 ISBN-10: 1-4296-1194-4 (softcover pbk.)
 1. Apples—Juvenile literature. 2. Orchards—Juvenile literature. 3. Apples. 4. Orchards. I. Title. II. Title:
Apple orchard. III. Series.
SB363.M8718 2008
634'.11—dc22   2006100173

Summary: Simple text and photos present a visit to an apple orchard—in both English and Spanish.

Interactive ISBN-13: 978-0-7368-7914-9
Interactive ISBN-10: 0-7368-7914-5

Editorial Credits

Sarah L. Schuette, editor; Katy Kudela, bilingual editor; translations.com, translation services; Eida del Risco,
    Spanish copy editor; Enoch Peterson, book designer; Jennifer Bergstrom, set designer

Photo Credits

Capstone Press / Gary Sundermeyer, all

The author thanks Bob Quig at Quig's Apple Orchard, in Mundelein, Illionis, and Michael Berst of the Apple
Journal for research assistance. She dedicates this book to Erik and Olivia.

Capstone Press thanks Topper and the staff of Sponsel's Minnesota Harvest Orchard in Jordan, Minnesota, and
Welsh Heritage Farms in Lake Crystal, Minnesota, for assistance with photo shoots.

Note to Parents and Teachers

The Una visita a / A Visit to set supports national social studies standards related to the production, distribution, and consumption of goods and services. This book describes and illustrates a visit to an apple orchard in both English and Spanish. The images support early readers in understanding the text. The repetition of words and phrases helps early readers learn new words. This book also introduces early readers to subject-specific vocabulary words, which are defined in the Glossary section. Early readers may need assistance to read some words and to use the Table of Contents, Glossary, Internet Sites, and Index sections of the book.

Table of Contents

Tabla de contenidos

The Apple Orchard

Apples grow in apple orchards. An apple orchard is a tasty place to visit.

La huerta de manzanas

Las manzanas crecen en huertas de manzanas. Visitar una huerta de manzanas es un paseo sabroso.

Rows of apple trees grow
in orchards. Different kinds
of apples grow on different
kinds of apple trees.

En la huerta crecen filas de
manzanos. Los diferentes tipos
de manzanas crecen en tipos
de manzano distintos.

Picking Apples

Workers pick apples in fall.

They put apples into bags.

La cosecha de manzanas

Los trabajadores recogen las

manzanas en otoño.

Las colocan en bolsas.

Workers drive tractors.
The tractors pull wagons
filled with apples.

Los trabajadores manejan
tractores. Los tractores jalan
vagones llenos de manzanas.

Machines wash and
polish apples. The apples
move along belts in
a packing line.

Existen máquinas que lavan y
pulen las manzanas. Las manzanas
se mueven en bandas en la línea
de empaquetado.

13

Machines sort apples
by size. Workers pack
apples into crates.

Las máquinas separan las
manzanas por tamaño.
Los trabajadores empaquetan
las manzanas en cajones.

Eating Apples

Visitors can taste different
kinds of apples.

¡A comer manzanas!

Los visitantes pueden probar
los distintos tipos de manzanas.

CORTLAND   MCINTOSH

CONNELL RED

SELLI

Visitors shop at the apple store. They buy bags of apples, apple pies, cider, and other items.

Los visitantes pueden comprar en la tienda de la huerta. Compran bolsas de manzanas, pasteles de manzana, jugo de manzana y muchas cosas más.

Apple orchards grow
healthy snacks. An apple
orchard is a fun place
to visit.

Las huertas de manzanas cultivan
golosinas saludables. Visitar una
huerta de manzanas es un paseo
muy divertido.

Glossary

cider—a beverage made by pressing apples

crate—a large wooden box

orchard—a field or farm where fruit trees grow

polish—to rub to make shiny

sort—to arrange in a group; apples are sorted by size and color.

tractor—a heavy machine that is used to pull machinery and other heavy loads

wagon—a vehicle with wheels that is used to carry heavy loads

Glosario

el cajón—caja grande de madera

la huerta—campo o granja donde crecen árboles frutales

el jugo de manzana—bebida hecha al prensar las manzanas

pulir—frotar algo para que brille

separar—acomodar en grupos; las manzanas se separan por tamaño y por color

el tractor—vehículo de carga que se usa para jalar máquinas o cargas pesadas

el vagón—carro con ruedas que se usa para arrastrar cargas pesadas

Internet Sites

FactHound offers a safe, fun way to find Internet sites related to this book. All of the sites on FactHound have been researched by our staff.

Here's how:

1. Visit *www.facthound.com*

2. Choose your grade level.

3. Type in this book ID **1429600810** for age-appropriate sites. You may also browse subjects by clicking on letters, or by clicking on pictures and words.

4. Click on the **Fetch It** button.

FactHound will fetch the best sites for you!

Index

Sitios de Internet

FactHound te brinda una manera divertida y segura de encontrar sitios de Internet relacionados con este libro. Hemos investigado todos los sitios de FactHound. Es posible que algunos sitios no estén en español.

Se hace así:

1. Visita *www.facthound.com*

2. Elige tu grado escolar.

3. Introduce este código especial **1429600810** para ver sitios apropiados a tu edad, o usa una palabra relacionada con este libro para hacer una búsqueda general.

4. Haz un clic en el botón **Fetch It**.

¡FactHound buscará los mejores sitios para ti!

Índice

36562574
9/09 SP ENF 634 murphy

Stayton Public Library
515 North First Avenue
Stayton, Oregon 97383